IMAGES OF ENGLAND

Hythe

A Southern Railway poster for Hythe, calling it 'The Pride of Kent'.

IMAGES OF ENGLAND

Hythe

Joy Melville and Angela Lewis-Johnson

NONSUCH

Cover illustration: The 'Relief of Mafeking Celebrations', on 19 May 1900 in Hythe.

First published 1995
This new pocket edition 2005
Images unchanged from first edition

Nonsuch Publishing Limited
The Mill, Brimscombe Port,
Stroud, Gloucestershire, GL5 2QG
www.nonsuch-publishing.com

British Library Cataloguing in Publication Data.
A catalogue record for this book is available from the British Library.

ISBN 1-84588-153-2

Typesetting and origination by Nonsuch Publishing Limited
Printed in Great Britain by Oaklands Book Services Limited

Contents

You "Auto" come to HYTHE

'You AUTO come to HYTHE.' A punning advertisement card, from which spill out a number of miniature views of the town.

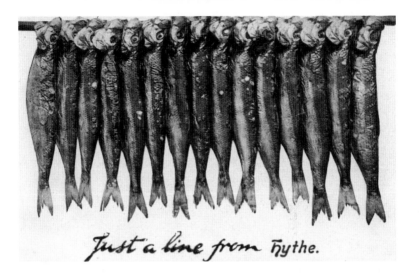

Just a line from Hythe.

Introduction

Hythe has always been a fighting town. One of the original Cinque Ports, it has long been a strategic part of England's military defences. Throughout the Middle Ages, the town fought against the French and when, in 1293, a French fleet sailed to attack Hythe, the townspeople set on it and murdered them all. Misfortune hit the townspeople in turn, later in the Middle Ages, when they suffered two visitations of the Black Death.

Despite shingle and silt blocking up the harbour and rendering it useless by late Tudor times, Hythe still remained an effective military source. Up to 15,000 soldiers were billeted in and around Hythe at the height of the Napoleonic wars. A School of Musketry was opened in 1853 and to be 'Hythe-trained' was regarded as a mark of excellence.

Wars apart, Hythe has a character all its own. It is a cliffside town, built in terraces up a steep hill, with splendid views out to the sea. And unlike most seaside resorts, within a mile or so you would think you were in the country, with sheep and lambs and tiny country inns.

The town has so many attractions, like the canal, winding its way through the town, with its boats and ducks and swans. Then there are its ornamental walks; the Norman church of St Leonard's, regarded as one of the finest in Kent; its miniature railway, and the eighteenth-century houses and inns around the ancient High Street.

Traffic tends to scream along the nearby motorway on its way to Dover and the Channel Tunnel, ignoring the sliproad to Hythe. This suits the locals very well, but passers-by are missing a still-fascinating town.

Joy Melville
Angela Lewis-Johnson
Hythe
Kent

The Town Bridge in 1829, an oasis of peace. Now, traffic on the new High Street bypass road roars by the end of the bridge.

Joy Melville and Angela Lewis-Johnson have both been associated with Hythe for a number of years. Joy has lived half in London and half in Hythe since the 1960s, while Angela, her cousin, lives in Hythe full-time. They are both enthusiastic about the town and have long collected postcards of its changing character.

Joy, who is an author, has written nine books. These include a biography of Ellen Terry, who lived at Smallhythe in Kent; and, published last year, *The Mother of Oscar*, a biography of Lady Wilde. Angela, who studied art at Goldsmith's College, London, has designed various local history books. These include *A Family Story: the life of Sir John Ruggles-Brise*, who was the Lord Lieutenant of Essex for 20 years.

Although the authors have their own collection of postcards of Hythe and its surrounds, they could never have compiled this book without the extreme generosity of a number of Hythe residents, who were willing to lend them their prized and private photographs. Both authors would particularly like to thank Molly and Sonny Griggs; Yvonne Bushell; Mr and Mrs Davison; Jack Barker; John Davies; Maurice Newman and Newman & Sons; Ralph Reesby, and The Hope Inn. Talking to such residents about their memories of Hythe in the old days was one of the added pleasures in compiling this book.

The local history room in the Hythe Library also has an attractively laid-out history of the town, with artefacts from its early days as a Cinque Port. It gives a comprehensive portrait of a unique town.

One

The Beach and Promenade

The Parade, Hythe

Strolling along the promenade in Hythe has always been one of the town's main pleasurable entertainments. But the sun to Victorians and Edwardians was an enemy, not friend, and was anxiously warded off by shady hats and parasols. In 1881, the Prince of Wales opened Hythe's new Marine Parade, called 'Prince's Parade.'

Before the First World War, bathing costumes were designed to reveal very little of the wearer. Sea bathing was regarded as a form of medical treatment, but the idea of removing one's clothes in public was unthinkable. Bathing huts provided the modest answer to this.

Well-to-do Victorians loved to spend their seaside holidays at Hythe. Dressed in their Sunday best, they would make excursions to Folkestone, where they were able to watch the arrival of the India Mail Boat from Boulogne.

'The new shelter on the sea front', says this card, posted in 1908. The Oriental design proved an attractive, shady alternative to being pushed along the promenade in a bathchair or taken by perambulator.

The Hythe beach is mainly shingle, deposited by the Channel current. It was one of the main reasons why the harbour silted-up, causing the town, centuries ago, to lose its claim to be a working Cinque Port.

The large wheels on the bathing tents enabled them to be driven into the sea so that bathers only had to go down the tent's few steps to be able to swim in relative privacy. The first bathing machine was used at Margate in 1750.

A relatively deserted sea-front, with visitors resting inside or alongside their bathing tents. From 1851 to 1914 Hythe remained about half way up the list of the 100 most popular seaside towns in Britain.

The building known as Moyle Tower acted as a Christian Holiday Centre in the 1920s and 1930s, attracting large numbers of Christian visitors to Hythe.

One of the main pleasures that the beach offered children in the 1920s and 1930s was a ride on a donkey. This is now missing, but adults still take a traditional Sunday stroll along the promenade.

Opposite above: The 1st Hythe B.P. Scout Troop was formed in 1908, not long after the launch of the scout movement. An instructive day by the sea gave scouts a chance to attain various 'seaworthy' proficiency badges.

Opposite below: The beach in the 1950s. The cult of sunworship began during the 1930s and exposure to the sea and sun became an increasingly and highly sought-after pleasure. Today, like the Victorians before us, we are once again aware of the sun's dangers.

When winds lash the sea around Hythe, waves often come right up and over the houses on the sea-front. Sandbags are a frequent sight.

On New Year's Day 1877, a mixture of strong winds and a Spring high tide on a weakened sea front caused extensive flooding. Hythe's impressive Imperial Hotel, above, built in 1880 and originally called the Seabrook Hotel, was virtually cut off.

Two

Around the High Street

High St Hythe West

For about 250 years Hythe's Town Hall was just a room above the Parish Church porch. In 1660 the Court Hall was erected, which combined being a court house with a market hall. A corn market was held weekly there from 1836 and this continued until the 1880s. The present Town Hall (above, right), on its white colonnades, was built on the site of the Court Hall in 1794.

High Street, Hythe.

Memories of the past in the High Street include the lanterns (above, left and right) which acted as useful advertisements for the contents of the shop and the Victorian lamplight (left). Shop-owners stand watching while carriages make their leisurely process down an almost empty street, past the parked delivery carts and traps.

Opposite above: The High Street in 1860, featuring the old Rose and Crown inn. A century earlier, it had been known as King's Street.

Opposite below: A busy shopping scene in the Edwardian High Street before cars came to crowd shoppers back on the pavements. It was said that 'the shops as well as the dwellings belonging to the superior classes of inhabitants speak the opulence, respectability and commercial importance of the place'.

The Jacobean Smugglers Retreat (on the left) in the High Street, once used as a fish shop, was a well-known landmark until it was demolished in 1908. The small tower in the roof was reputed to be where a lantern was placed, in order to signal to smugglers at sea. The infamous Ransley gang of smugglers was active around Hythe and the main contraband – hidden in underground cellars – was wine, spirits, tea, tobacco, lace, and silks.

The High Street in 1907, when delivery boys used bicycles or pony and traps and most shops had pull-down shades. The sign on the wall above the shoe shop reads, 'Boots and shoes for strong school wear'.

The lower, east end of the long, narrow High Street late last century, showing how many of the old shops and houses had fallen into disrepair.

The projecting Town Hall clock was erected in 1871 and dominates the High Street. A notice high up on the wall underneath it, which probably dates from the 1798 Hythe Paving Act, reads, 'All Persons are requested to unite their Endeavours to keep this Place clean and to prevent BOYS or others from dirting the same'.

The Hope Inn, in Stade Street, a road leading to the shore from the High Street, dates back to 1790. It was used then as an Officers' Mess by the military on alert to stop Napoleon's threatened invasion. In 1827, the newly licensed premises were called The Hope Inn, probably in honour of General Alexander Hope who had been active in local defence fortifications in and around Hythe during 1809.

While the military were in Hythe, there was never a shortage of inns for them to visit.

In a rearguard action, temperance hotels offered travellers an alternative to hard drinking. On the right of the hotel, seen here in the early part of this century, a notice from the Congregational Church invites passers-by to attend Divine Service.

Market Square at the top end of the High Street, acted as a centre of transport. The carriages on the left wait for passengers, while, centre, more horses are held at the ready by the stables. The horse-drawn carrier on the right wends his way from the square loaded up with baskets, while behind him on the corner is the old teashop.

MARKET SQUARE, HYTHE.

The Folkestone/Sandgate/Hythe Tramway opened in 1892 and passengers were pulled along by pairs of horses harnessed to single carriages. Above, left, the tram, with a clearly displayed route, waits for passengers outside the Red Lion Hotel.

Market Square, Hythe, looking East.

Two trams wait in Market Square, which was renamed Red Lion Square after the hotel, seen here on the right.

At the lower end of the High Street stood the old watermill, run by the Burch family for nearly a century and sold in 1932. It was said that smugglers hid their casks of brandy in the mill stream.

The attraction of the tiny lanes leading from the High Street up the steep hillside alongside the church lies in the enchanting old houses and cottages, with flowers growing from window-boxes and hanging baskets. Traffic still squeezes alongside Georgian houses and small alleyways.

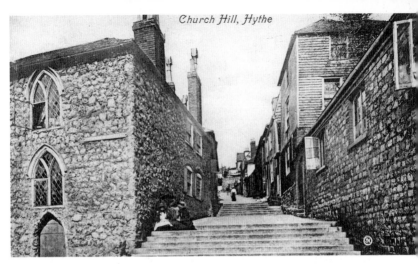

The steep steps of Church Hill now have a railing going up the centre to help breathless climbers. Elizabeth Bowen, the novelist, once lived here. And on the left, on the corner of Church Hill and Bartholomew Street, is the twelfth-century house, 'Centuries,' said to be the birthplace of the Bishop of Rochester in 1275.

A side-view of 'Centuries' showing its arched windows and entrance. It was renovated in 1811 and has been used as an almshouse.

Sun Lane, one of the peaceful lanes off the High Street, in 1930.

The reality of battle is brought home by this tank, situated for a time next to the war memorial, near the canal.

Opposite above: Theatre Street, off the High Street, with its distinctive white shutters on the houses. The theatre itself used to stand on the extreme left.

Opposite below: The attractive arched windows of St John's Hospital at the lower end of the High Street.

Bank Street, one of the major streets leading to the High Street, in 1924. 'Hythe is such a lovely old town', says the writer of the postcard.

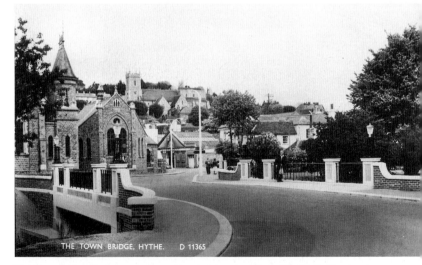

THE TOWN BRIDGE, HYTHE.   D 11365

The Town Bridge, Hythe, spans the canal and gives a clear view of the Methodist church.

Marine Walk Street, off the High Street, in 1915. Advertisements for Fry's Chocolate and Cadbury's Chocolate plaster the front of the small corner shop. The neat ninetenth-century terraced houses on the right face one of Hythe's typically old, white clapboard houses on the left of the street.

Stade Street used to be the only road going down to the seashore and boasted no fewer than four windmills. Here it is seen in 1918.

Above: Although East Street is at the end of the High Street, it gives a decidedly rural impression.

Left: One of the many attractive narrow streets, with its distinctive clapboard houses, leading on to the High Street.

Above: The mock Tudor shop bought by Newman's, the furniture company, in 1951, and which closed in February 1995. Before that the shop, which has twice suffered fires, had only changed hands once this century.

Right: Ready to go off on a jaunt, outside the Bushell Boot Warehouse in the High Street.

Above, Oddfellows Hall at the bottom of the High Street. Oddfellows was one of the many benevolent societies formed in the early part of the nineteenth century.

Three

The Royal Military Canal

HYTHE CANAL

Shaded by trees, and with pathways on both sides, the Royal Military Canal gives Hythe much of its character.

Hythe in 1816, showing the military barracks and the canal, which had recently been cut. After war was declared with France in 1793 there was a lively fear for a decade that Napoleon would invade England with his vast flotilla of boats. The construction of a Royal Military Canal was on the orders of William Pitt. Work started in 1803 and Pitt supervised much of the work. The original plan was to make it 60 feet wide at the top, nine feet deep and some 25 miles long. It was to be defended by cannon and small forts reached from inland behind a tall earth bank.

Looking at the peaceful scenery of the canal, it is hard to imagine that it was built for war.

The ornamental gardens on both banks of the canal were at their best in the 1880s, but even seventy years later they retained their beauty, as they still do today.

Pleasure boating on the canal became popular during the latter part of the nineteenth century. The canal had been officially opened to public navigation in 1810, though passage boats had to pay toll. For years the canal was used to transport light cargo like coal, timber, produce and shingle.

The boating scene in 1910, with the boats neatly lined up alongside the boathouse.

Feeding the ducks and swans that glide up and down the canal is a favourite activity for adults as well as for children.

The reason the canal was designed to follow a zigzag course was so that cannons could be strategically placed at each angle.

The Duke's Head Bridge, pictured here in 1910. Originally only wooden bridges were erected over the canal as all the bricks were needed for building the impressive line of Martello Towers along the coastline.

The war memorial, surrounded by a flower garden, was erected next to the old bandstand, which was later gutted by fire.

Looking at the ageless peace of the canal, one forgets the hardships its building caused. It was difficult for workmen to find accommodation for their wives, and the *Kentish Gazette* in 1805 reported that the wife of one of the workmen cutting the canal 'was conducted by her husband to the market place at Hythe with a halter round her neck and tied to a post, from when she was purchased for sixpence by a mulatto'.

Beginning in 1860 and with gaps only during wars, Hythe has held a summer pageant, or water festival, on the canal. Called the Venetian Fête, and now held every two years, a procession of decorated floats come down the canal in daylight, then returned, illuminated, after sunset. H.G. Wells described the Venetian Fête in Kipps.

The Pride of Hythe caravan, advocating 'Tita Kontrol', was manned by members of the Newman family like all three floats featured on these pages.

Above, a float in the shape of a crown to commemorate the Queen's coronation.

The Avenue, one of the attractive walks near to the canal. It is hard to realise that the sea is only a few hundred yards away.

The Grove, in 1911. The Victorians, who planned much of the area around the canal, thought that it was important for gardens to be recreational as well as ornamental.

48

Four

The Ladies' Walk

The Marine or Ladies' Walk.

The Ladies' Walk was originally a footpath down to the seashore, laid out to commemorate the Jubilee of George III in 1810. It was flanked with elm trees, like the canal itself.

Troops who attended training courses at the School of Musketry in the 1880s could take part in 'boating and bathing and cricket in the pretty little ground by the Ladies Walk'.

It was the demands of the Victorian seaside holidays which lay behind the original development of these shaded walks.

The Ladies' Walk as it appeared in January 1877, when it was inundated by the sea.

Over the years, the scenery of Ladies' Walk has changed as trees initially grew thicker, and then were felled. Now, many of these trees have disappeared. But for residents of Hythe it remains a favourite walk, linking the town to the sea.

Left: The Ladies' Walk Bridge, over the canal, was built in 1813 to connect the town with Ladies' Walk. It was swept away by the encroaching sea at the time of the great flood on 1 January 1877.

Below: Walking had its drawbacks in lanes made muddy by rain.

Five

The Parish Church

The parish church of St Leonard's, seen here in 1750. It was built by the Normans around 1080 on the site of a stone Saxon church, and virtually soars over the town owing to its commanding position on a steep hill.

Among those who are buried in the old churchyard is Lionel Lukin, the inventor in 1785 of the first lifeboat.

Inside the church, the most remarkable feature is the high chancel, built around 1220, which rises above the nave of the original Norman church. The great east window dominates the inside of the church.

The vaulted crypt, or ambulatory, of St Leonard's is lined like a catacombe with a remarkable collection of what are said to be some 2,000 skulls and 8,000 thighbones. There is only one other similar collection in England.

CRYPT OF HYTHE CHURCH

The origin of the skulls is not known, though they are thought to be of people living between Norman times and that of Queen Elizabeth I. One theory is that they are bones dug up to make room for victims of the recurrent Black Death.

PARISH CHURCH, HYTHE.

The Font, Hythe Churc...

Above: A collection of the attractions of St Leonard's church, possibly including the clergyman?

Left: The original font was probably destroyed by the Puritans. Over the years, it has been moved to different positions around the church. Its bowl is fourteenth century, while the stem dates from the nineteenth century. Its fine wooden canopy is no longer used.

An aerial view of St Leonard's church, showing its dominating position in the town.

The High Altar of the Catholic church in Hythe. The church was built in 1893 at a cost of about two and a half thousand pounds, to cater for the increasing number of Catholics.

St Michael's church, built in 1893, is a pale corrugated-iron building, nicknamed 'the mission church'. It was regarded as a working-man's church, for those 'shy of attending their parish church' or unable to reach it easily.

Six

Military Men

Marchers celebrate the centenary of the Hythe School of Musketry. The School opened in 1853 when a corps of instructors in musketry was formed to train officers in the use of the new Enfield rifle.

Hythe in 1824, showing the old barracks on the Old Barrack Ground. When William Cobbett visited Hythe in the 1820s, he wrote in his Rural Rides that 'Hythe itself is half barracks; the hills are covered in barracks; and barracks most expensive, most squandering, fill up the side of the hill'.

The substantial brick buildings of the School of Musketry, erected by the government in 1807-8. Besides apartments for officers, there was accommodation for about 300 men and rooms for married soldiers. In 1919, after muskets were superseded by other weapons, the name was changed to the Small Arms Wing. This School of Infantry left Hythe in 1968 and moved to Warminster in Wiltshire.

Inside the lecture room of the School of Musketry.

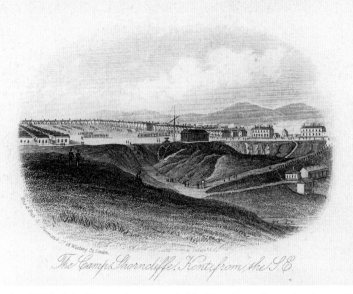

The Camp Shorncliffe, Kent, from the S.E.

In October 1802 Sir John Moore, who commanded the Kent district, began planning a training camp at Shorncliffe, along the coast from Hythe.

Cavalry Guardsman outside Shorncliffe Camp. Such military establishments in the area became training camps for thousands of British and Canadian soldiers.

A line-up of horses and gun carriages at Shorncliffe Camp in 1909.

Impressive rows of soldiers being paraded in 1907, alongside their tents. The area has been called 'a militarised wasteland'.

In 1804, 88 Martello Towers with 11 or 18 pounder guns were constructed along the coast. The entrance was 10 feet above ground level; the ground floor contained the magazine and storerooms; and the middle floor had room for an officer and 24 men. The soldiers manning these sea batteries were expected to "annoy" the enemy while they were landing and prevent them from unloading stores.

In peacetime, one Martello Tower on the Hythe seafront was turned into a striking but comfortable house.

Seven

Neighbouring Villages

Just outside Hythe, and visible from the town, is the stretch of countryside known to local people as 'the Roughs'. It possibly traces an older coastline.

Lympne, on the outskirts of Hythe, was one of the forts the Romans built against Saxon pirates and Vikings in the third century. Lympne Castle, rebuilt in Medieval times, was restored early this century. It stands on high land, with superb views across the farmlands of Romney Marsh.

Next to Lympne Castle stands a Medieval church, looking as much like a fortress as the castle. Its Norman tower was built about 1100. The path down from the castle goes past the remaining fragments of the fort.

Above: Redbrooks, near Hythe, is delightfully rural with wild flowers, like bluebells, adding to its enchantment.

Right: Redbrooks has always been a favourite playground for children.

Saltwood Castle.

Saltwood lies way up above Hythe, half a mile north of the town. This view is north-east from Kiln Cottage Corner, showing the Castle and the line of the Downs.

22 SALTWOOD. — The Village Green (Near Hythe). — LL.

The centre of the village of Saltwood, showing a traditional small village green and a long-since vanished pond.

Saltwood Castle.

The Normans built a castle on the site of one said to have been built by the son of Hengist in 488. It has been restored many times before falling into a romantic, semi-ruin. Its impressive fourteenth-century gatehouse was lived in by the art historian Sir Kenneth Clark. In December 1170, four knights, Fitzurze, de Tracy, de Moreville, and le Bret, left the castle for Canterbury to assassinate the archbishop Thomas à Becket.

The picturesque, Medieval Saltwood church.

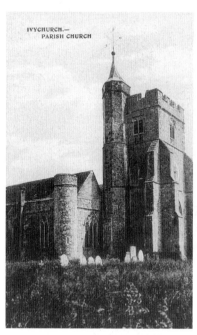

IVYCHURCH.—
PARISH CHURCH

Left: The churches on Romney Marsh were often used by smugglers to hide their contraband. Once, the service at the church at Ivychurch had to be cancelled, as so many brandy kegs and tobacco were stored away under the flooring in the north aisle.

Below: This cottage is so smothered in greenery it illustrates how Ivychurch got its name.

Ponies and traps wait peacefully for their owners outside the Gardner & Company Inn at Sellinge, a village near Hythe on the road to Ashford.

Hythe's natural harbour, which became silted-up, was originally formed by a creek which cut inland to West Hythe. Above, the ruins of West Hythe church.

A farm at Aldington, a village renowned in the sixteenth century for housing Elizabeth Barton, believed to be divinely inspired, and known as the Holy Maid of Kent. Unfortunately for her, she prophesied disaster if Henry VIII should divorce Catherine of Aragon, and as a result she died on the scaffold.

Slaybrook, an old listed building in the countryside near Hythe, seen here in 1906.

Right: Monks Horton lies a little way off the Hythe road. Kite Cottage, right, is one of its beautiful Tudor manor houses, with an oriel window, kingpost, and fine carved overmantel. One of the rebels beheaded with Sir Thomas Wyatt lived at the priory here and turned towards the place on the scaffold, saying 'Surely you will let a dying Kentish man breathe the air of his beloved county?'

Below: The church at Old Romney, where sheep grazed right up to the door, is dedicated to St Clement, who was martyred by being drowned in the sea with an anchor tied round his neck. Legend has it that the sea then receded three miles to reveal the saint's body in a stone chest, with the anchor alongside.

Old Romney Church.

Sandgate, a small coastal resort next to Hythe, in 1906. Its high street, a step away from the sea, can get pounded by high seas.

The parade at Sandgate, in more peaceful weather. Many of the resort's old buildings were timbered, some with wooden balconies and shutters. H.G. Wells came to live here in 1899.

Above: Sandgate Castle on the seafront, originally part of Henry VIII's coastal defence scheme, has been so damaged by both sea and war that basically only the central tower is left.

Right: The stairs in the gate-tower of the castle.

The Stairs in the Gate-Tower of Sandgate Castle, showing entrance to the Small Museum.

Castle Copyright, No. 21.

Stanford, a small village at the top of the hill leading down to Hythe, now lies in two parts, bisected by the motorway.

Ponies and traps waiting outside the old Forge and Drum Inn at Stanford, in 1913.

An aerial view of Hythe, which has had the effect of giving its steep hillsides a curiously flattened look.

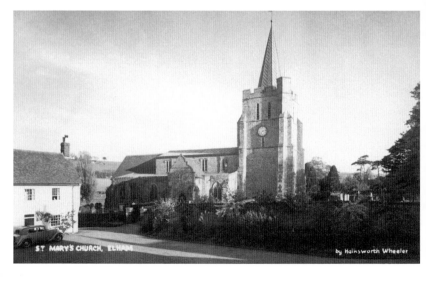

ST. MARY'S CHURCH, ELHAM

by Hainsworth Wheeler

The West Garden at Port Lympne, a mansion built in 1913 for Sir Philip Sassoon. Its 300 acres of park and woodland are now the home of rare and endangered species of animals.

Opposite above: Kent is rightly called the Garden of England. Above, a mass of primroses in Sandling Park Wood near Hythe.

Opposite below: St Mary's Church, Elham, a grey mass of stone, is over 700 years old. Alabaster carvings inside include those of Thomas à Becket and his assassins and figures in the chancel windows include Carlyle, Gladstone, and Disraeli.

The old Dungeness lighthouse was built in the early part of this century, but is now no longer in use. The Dungeness coast grows annually by several feet: the new lighthouse was built in 1960.

Eight

Romney, Hythe and Dymchurch Railway

The miniature Romney, Hythe and Dymchurch railway, with a gauge of 15 inches and called 'the smallest public railway in the world', was opened on 16 July 1927 by the Lord Warden of Cinque Ports, in full regalia. Using steam locomotives, it travels some 14 miles across the marshes to Romney. Here one of its engines can be seen positively dwarfed by the Argyll and Sutherland Highlanders.

Hurricane Engine at Hythe World Smallest Railway

Above: The Hurricane engine used on the railway.

Left: The back of the above card, written in 1930, says, 'This train was made, designed and belongs to Capt Howey and it is he that is standing by the engine. He is at Hythe every morning ... and during the busy season he always drives this, his first made, named *Hurricane*'. Early in 1925, Captain Howey, a railway enthusiast, looked for a site on which to build a public railway, intending to lay a single line, inspired by the growth of the first big holiday camps and shanty bungalows. The bus company was implacably opposed to it and the land-owners unsuccessfully complained their potential building sites were reduced in value by the noise of the railway. It retains its popularity to this day, attracting hoards of children.

Above, the Duke of York, later George VI, becomes the first official passenger in 1926. The railway was taken over for military use in June 1940 for the duration of the war.

A single-track line branched off the London to Dover rail link, running close to Saltwood Castle on its way to Hythe Station. Trains ran to the station, above, for 77 years until it was closed by Beeching cuts in 1951. Its closure was a real loss to Hythe, the nearest station now being located at Sandling.

Nine

Work and Play

One of the main attractions of Hythe is that it is both a rural and seaside resort, offering unlimited opportunities for country as well as seafront walks.

Clyne House in North Road, Hythe, the home of the Bushell family, whose children are seen in the next few pages. The photographs were all taken by William Bushell earlier this century.

A small garden house of the kind beloved by children and ideal for picnics.

Right: A ladder of Bushell children in the garden.

Below: Feeding the hens in the henhouse: a favourite occupation for youngsters.

Hythe firemen, carrying out the first trial practice with the fire engine.

Fire brigade drill, with hose-pipes flying in all directions and a row of interested watchers.

Right: Not saved in time. The burnt-out remains of the Sportsman Inn, Hythe.

Below: Lighting the fire under the suspended kettle is a delight for small boys.

The magnificent acres of azaleas, magnolias and rhododendrons of the Garden House at Saltwood were shaped by colonies of beavers around the time the Romans left Britain.

The gardeners have a full-time job looking after the many shrubs and trees.

The 'Relief of Mafeking' Celebrations, which took place in Hythe on 19 May 1900. The sign reads 'Torchlight Procession and Bonfire Tonight', and the whole town turned out.

The Mackeson Hythe Brewery Cricket Club, ready for action in 1928. The famous milk stout was first produced in 1907.

The canal was stocked with tench in 1806. Fishing has long been a favourite activity in Hythe.

Beating the bounds at Hythe on 5 October 1910.

The Bowling Green at Hythe. Bowls have been played at Hythe since the Bowling Club took in its first members in 1655.

Speech-time at Empire Day celebrations on Hythe Green in the year 1911. The scouts band is on the right.

Empire Day celebrations were taken very seriously. The watching children were all given a day off school and expected to participate.

The staff pictured in front of the building of the Metropole Steam Laundry Co. Ltd in the Dymchurch Road early this century. On the right is the horse-drawn delivery van. The laundry continued to operate right up to the Second World War, but closed shortly after.

Relaxing around the old bandstand near the canal in the 1920s.

The colourful Hythe Town Excelsior Military Band, founded in 1900.

The Band of the 1st Cinque Ports Royal Garrison Artillery Volunteers. Most of the band consisted of local men and the bandmaster was J.H.C. Nelson.

The sign at the bottom of the photograph, concealing one boy's lace-up shoes, reads 'Hythe School, 1907, Group 2'. The Hythe School for Boys, in Prospect Place, was a private, fee-paying school.

Opposite above: Vegetable and flower shows have always played an important part in local life.

Opposite below: Children show as much interest as the adults at the Palmarsh flower show of 1955.

Hospital Sunday, August 1910. The Hythe Town Band leads the parade, with banners held aloft behind them.

A blinkered donkey at work pulling a cart.

Ten

Driving Around

The Folkestone and District Bus in 1918, bowling along at Sandgate on its way to Hythe.

The Toast Rack, at Hythe Terminus.

A horse-drawn tram at the Hythe terminal in Red Lion Square. The Folkestone, Sandgate and Hythe Tramways Company started a service from Hythe to Sandgate in 1892. A tram-shed housing trams and horses was built in 1894 and remained there until 1922, when the service ended. Evidence of the tramlines remained in the cobbles of the forecourt.

The Toast Rack, 5 Miles by the Sea, Sandgate, Seabrook & Hythe.

All set for the three-mile drive from Hythe to Sandgate. Because of the way the passengers were seated, the horse-drawn trams were nicknamed 'toast-racks'. In the winter, to help counter the weather, they were glass-sided.

Newman's, who hired out traps and acted as carriers and removers, also ran this station bus. The sign on the top of the bus, pictured in Douglas Avenue in the 1930s, reads, 'Hythe Station Bus: to all parts of the district'.

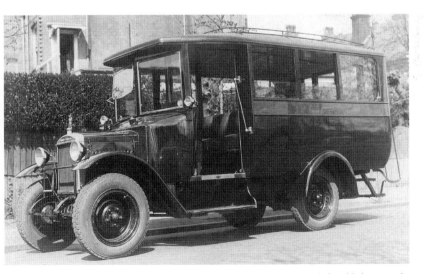

The station bus was virtually a taxi service. Nowadays it seems to us an unbelievable luxury to be able to summon a bus to call at our door and take us and our luggage to the station.

The driver at the wheel of this charabanc, seen here aged 18 in 1928, was later to become Mayor of Hythe.

A Studebaker hearse in front of a mourning car, an Austin taxi, in Prospect Road in the late 1920s. Both were run by Newmans.

The funeral of a former police sergeant wends its impressive way on the road from Seabrook, the next village to Hythe, in 1924. Members of the Kent police force accompany the flower-bedecked hearse and line up behind the last carriage.

Two members of the Newman family, for so long associated with Hythe, stroll along in Red Lion Square in the late 1930s. .

Opposite above: Two taxis and a coach wait for hire in Newman's Garage, opposite the Salvation Army Hall. The area is now a school playground.

Opposite below: Coaches on a Newman family firm outing in 1938. They are parked outside Church House, which was used for various local activities like plays.

'Ask for Whitbreads Ales and Stout' says the sign on the brewery van. Painted on the door is 'Agents, Mackeson and Co. Ltd, Hythe'. Whitbread bought up Mackeson's in 1929.

This particular van was decorated for the United Friendly Societies' Hospital Carnival, in which it won first prize.

Eleven

The Sea: friend and foe

Becalmed Fishing Boat.

Fishermen everywhere are dependent for their livelihood on the mood of the sea. Fishing in Hythe has always been one of its main industries.

It's not enough merely to catch the fish, it also has to be sold. Here, fish from the 'Live Fish' cart is weighed out for a customer earlier this century.

The fish delivery and selling barrow in St Leonard's Road. Many a Hythe resident can still remember this.

Sonny Griggs of Hythe working with his trawl net. He has spent a lifetime as a fisherman.

Fishermen in a rare moment of relaxation, lean against their boat.

'Mackerel seining' in Hythe. The fish are trapped in the net when the ends are brought together and have to be laboriously and carefully shaken out.

A photo of the fisherman William Griggs, who died in 1889, at the back of the family home in Stade Street.

FISHERMEN'S BEACH HYTHE

Above: This part of the beach at Hythe, looking towards Dymchurch, is known as Fisherman's Beach. Fish is still sold there today after the boats come in with their overnight catch.

Left: The Three Brothers, pictured here about 1900, was one of a fleet of colliers which plied between Hartlepool and Hythe, landing coal for the town. In winter, when the beach at Hythe was inaccessible, the coal was landed at Folkestone and taken by pony and cart to Hythe.

Toby Griggs, known as the Father of the Lifeboat.

As with fishing, being lifeboatmen runs in the family. Often the two activities are combined. Here, pictured in 1928, Toby Griggs and his four sons, John, Sonny, Buller and Dick.

The crew of the new motorised lifeboat the *City of Nottingham*, the latest design for the time. The lifeboat was presented by Nottingham and named after it.

The *City of Nottingham* crew seen here hauling hard on the ropes to move their boat.

The doors of the lifeboat house are opened for the launch of the lifeboat.

The old Hythe lifeboat, called *Meyer de Rothschild*, was the last one that used sail and oars.

The crew of the *City of Nottingham* in 1934 in front of the original lifeboat house. Alongside the new lifeboat (right) is the old *Meyer de Rothschild*.

The lifeboat that went to the aid of the sinking ship, *Benvenue*, in 1891, being towed by horse through Sandgate. The lifeboat was launched three times and 27 survivors were rescued. One lifeboatman was drowned and Wright Griggs, standing third from left, was one of those awarded the Silver Medal by the RNLI.

Townspeople early this century congregate to look at the lifeboat.

Years later, they show an equal interest in the lifeboat, *The Viscountess Wakefield*.

Behind the family in the boat are the remains of two decoy piers, erected during the Second World War to confuse the Germans.

Fishermen mend their nets, broken by the nearby engine of a Spitfire which came down in the Channel during the war.

Part of a Wellington bomber and its Hythe rescuers after the plane, shot in a bombing raid over Milan, crashed in the sea near to Hythe. The lifeboat was launched immediately to bring back survivors.

The sea itself can be an enemy. Hythe townspeople have had to survive some hurricane-force storms over the centuries.

The force of the waves has smashed the seafront on a number of occasions. This photograph was taken early in the century but the 1987 hurricane also left a trail of destruction in the town.

The band, watched by onlookers, on what was named Titanic Sunday. The intention was to collect money for the survivors of the Titanic disaster.

The South Road and Parade houses in Hythe after being inundated by the sea in the great flood of 1877.

The old post mill at Hythe, which was removed from the town some time before the 1840s and taken a distance of nine miles by barge along the canal where it was re-erected at Ruckinge.